Sacred Solos
Level Five
Supplement to All Piano and Keyboard Methods
Arranged by Joan Cupp

Joan Cupp's musical ear and gift for improvising were discovered by her first grade teacher, who encouraged her to take piano lessons. Later, at age nine, young Joan had a memory lapse while playing Durand's "Waltz in E-flat" at a recital. Unfazed, she continued playing by improvising the next sixteen measures before returning to the original theme. She was applauded for her uninterrupted performance.

Joan Cupp is now a very successful private teacher of piano, organ, and synthesizer in Shirley, Indiana. She maintains a full schedule of teaching along with being a church musician. Her own natural talent for keyboard improvisation has been developed through vast experience in entertainment and church work. She currently teaches improvising, including pop, country-western, and gospel styles. Her 46 years of experience include performing with professional groups on radio, TV, and in recording studios.

Mrs. Cupp is co-author of *Keyboard Teaching with Greater Success and Satisfaction* and author of the Schaum *Music Teacher's Organizer*. She has conducted over 200 piano teacher seminars throughout the United States. She has been involved in contest work as a judge, accompanist, and teacher, with many of her students achieving high honors. Mrs. Cupp studied music at Ball State University (Muncie, Indiana) and organ at the Jordan Conservatory of Music (Indianapolis).

Contents

To access audio visit:
www.halleonard.com/mylibrary
Enter Code
5865-9353-7593-1333

ISBN 978-1-4950-8219-1

Schaum

EXCLUSIVELY DISTRIBUTED BY

Hal•Leonard®

Copyright © 2001 by Schaum Publications, Inc.
International Copyright Secured   All Rights Reserved

For all works contained herein:
Unauthorized copying, arranging, adapting, recording, Internet posting, public performance,
or other distribution of the music in this publication is an infringement of copyright.
Infringers are liable under the law.

Visit Hal Leonard Online at
www.halleonard.com

Contact us:
Hal Leonard
7777 West Bluemound Road
Milwaukee, WI 53213
Email: info@halleonard.com

In Europe, contact:
Hal Leonard Europe Limited
42 Wigmore Street
Marylebone, London, W1U 2RN
Email: info@halleonardeurope.com

In Australia, contact:
Hal Leonard Australia Pty. Ltd.
4 Lentara Court
Cheltenham, Victoria, 3192 Australia
Email: info@halleonard.com.au

Amazing Grace

Espressivo ♩ = 80 - 92

Early American Melody

Blessed Assurance
What a Friend We Have In Jesus

Phoebe P. Knapp
C.C. Converse

Holy, Holy, Holy

John B. Dykes

It Is Well With My Soul

Philip P. Bliss

Andante con espressivo ♩ = 88-100

Sweet Hour of Prayer

William B. Bradbury

* **15ᵐᵃ** means to play **two octaves higher** than written.

Crown Him With Many Crowns
My Faith Looks Up To Thee

George J. Elvey
Lowell Mason

In The Garden

Teneramente

C. Austin Miles

Meno Mosso ♩= 92

Just a Closer Walk with Thee

Anonymous

* 8th notes played as ♫ = ♪♪♪

Stand Up, Stand Up for Jesus

Maestoso ♩ = 92 - 104

George J. Webb

Performance Note: If desired, some or all of the bass notes indicated with octave lower signs may be played as octaves. Form the octave by playing the note in the staff with a note one octave lower.

MORE GREAT SCHAUM PUBLICATIONS

FINGERPOWER®

by John W. Schaum

Physical training and discipline are needed for both athletics and keyboard playing. Keyboard muscle conditioning is called technique. technique exercises are as important to the keyboard player as workouts and calisthenics are to the athlete. Schaum's *Fingerpower®* books are dedicated to development of individual finger strength and dexterity in both hands.

00645334	Primer Level – Book Only	$7.99
00645016	Primer Level – Book/Audio	$9.99
00645335	Level 1 – Book Only	$6.99
00645019	Level 1 – Book/Audio	$8.99
00645336	Level 2 – Book Only	$7.99
00645022	Level 2 – Book/Audio	$9.99
00645337	Level 3 – Book Only	$6.99
00645025	Level 3 – Book/Audio	$7.99
00645338	Level 4 – Book Only	$6.99
00645028	Level 4 – Book/Audio	$9.99
00645339	Level 5 Book Only	$7.99
00645340	Level 6 Book Only	$7.99

FINGERPOWER® ETUDES

Melodic exercises crafted by master technique composers. Modified or transposed etudes provide equal hand development with a planned variety of technical styles, keys, and time signatures.

00645392	Primer Level	$6.99
00645393	Level 1	$6.99
00645394	Level 2	$6.99
00645395	Level 3	$6.99
00645396	Level 4	$6.99

FINGERPOWER® FUN

arr. Wesley Schaum
Early Elementary Level

Musical experiences beyond the traditional *Fingerpower®* books that include fun-to-play pieces with finger exercises and duet accompaniments. Short technique preparatory drills (finger workouts) focus on melodic patterns found in each piece.

00645126	Primer Level	$6.95
00645127	Level 1	$6.99
00645128	Level 2	$6.95
00645129	Level 3	$6.99
00645144	Level 4	$6.95

FINGERPOWER® POP

arr. by James Poteat

10 great pop piano solo arrangements with fun technical warm-ups that complement the *Fingerpower®* series! Can also be used as motivating supplements to any method and in any learning situation.

00237508	Primer Level	$9.99
00237510	Level 1	$9.99
00282865	Level 2	$9.99
00282866	Level 3	$9.99
00282867	Level 4	$10.99

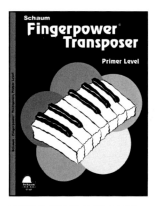

FINGERPOWER® TRANSPOSER

by Wesley Schaum
Early Elementary Level

This book includes 21 short, 8-measure exercises using 5-finger patterns. Positions are based on C,F, and G major and no key signatures are used. Patterns involve intervals of 3rds, 4ths, and 5ths up and down and are transposed from C to F and F to C, C to G and G to C, G to F and F to G.

00645150	Primer Level	$6.95
00645151	Level 1	$6.95
00645152	Level 2	$6.95
00645154	Level 3	$6.95
00645156	Level 4	$6.99

JUMBO STAFF MANUSCRIPT BOOK

This pad features 24 pages with 4 staves per page.

00645936 .... $4.25

CERTIFICATE OF MUSICAL ACHIEVEMENT

Reward your students for their hard work with these official 8x10-inch certificates that you can customize. 12 per package.

00645938 .... $6.99

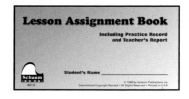

SCHAUM LESSON ASSIGNMENT BOOK

by John Schaum

With space for 32 weeks, this book will help keep students on the right track for their practice time.

00645935 .... $3.95

www.halleonard.com

Prices, contents, and availability subject to change without notice.